D1526644

THE CALL OF DUTY
CAREERS IN THE
ARMED FORCES™

YOUR CAREER IN THE
AIR FORCE

JERI FREEDMAN

ROSEN
PUBLISHING®

New York

In memory of my stepfather, First Lieutenant Vincent Jardine, 1930–2010, U.S. Air Force pilot

Published in 2012 by The Rosen Publishing Group, Inc.
29 East 21st Street, New York, NY 10010

Copyright © 2012 by The Rosen Publishing Group, Inc.

First Edition

Library of Congress Cataloging-in-Publication Data

Freedman, Jeri.
Your career in the Air Force / Jeri Freedman.—1st ed.
    p. cm.—(The call of duty: careers in the armed forces)
Includes bibliographical references and index.
ISBN 978-1-4488-5513-1 (library binding)
1. United States. Air Force—Juvenile literature. 2. United States. Air Force—Vocational guidance—Juvenile literature. I. Title.
UG633.F73 2012
358.40023'73—dc22
                                                    2011012006

Manufactured in the United States of America

CPSIA Compliance Information: Batch #W12YA: For further information, contact Rosen Publishing, New York, New York, at 1-800-237-9932.

CONTENTS

INTRODUCTION

With the wind whipping around him, Air Force pararescue jumper Alex clipped his waist harness onto a cord, braced his feet on the open doorway of the Pave Hawk helicopter and pushed backward into the void above New Orleans for the umpteenth time.

He dangled in the air, spinning slowly, as he descended about 60 feet alongside a three-story brick housing project north of the Louisiana Superdome. The pilot, Capt. Adam, kept the rescue helicopter hovering precariously close to the building, which is surrounded by floodwaters.

Alex landed gingerly on the roof of a dark-blue Chevrolet Suburban adrift next to the building. Then, in an agile, Spider-Man-like maneuver, he leapt from the car onto a nearby balcony and disappeared, going to the aid of a woman they spotted there moments earlier . . .

"This is what we live for," said flight engineer Staff Sgt. Peter, who mans the specialized hoist that lifts the flood victims and their rescuers to safety.

—Ann Scott Tyson, *Washington Post*, September 8, 2005

A pararescueman from the U.S. Air Force 38th Rescue Squadron rescues a child from a flooded house in New Orleans, Louisiana, after Hurricane Katrina.

During Hurricane Katrina, air force pararescue teams rescued thousands of people in the Gulf Coast from the flooding. They used helicopters equipped with infrared sensors that allowed them to locate survivors. This is just one of many real-life examples of careers in today's exciting and high-tech U.S. Air Force.

People join the air force for many reasons. Many see it as a way to pay for college or gain the skills to qualify for a high-paying technical career. Others seek adventure and the chance to work with high-tech equipment and aircraft. Yet others feel pride and satisfaction from doing something important, serving their country, and helping their fellow Americans.

There are many benefits that come from being in the military, including tuition reimbursement during and after service; the opportunity to learn valuable technical skills and gain an associate's degree; excellent health and dental care; free or subsidized housing; and generous vacations. Members of the air force get thirty days of vacation and can fly to a variety of destinations for free on air force aircraft with available space. Destinations include Italy, England, Germany, Japan, Australia, and most of the United States.

However, there are drawbacks. You may find yourself doing dangerous work, or you may be stationed in a war zone where your life is at risk. Also, military life may not suit everyone. When you join the armed forces, you must be prepared to give up a certain amount of personal freedom. You will have little control over your assignments or where you are sent to work. You should carefully consider the pros and cons before making the decision to join the air force.

If you decide you are interested in joining, be aware that air force operations primarily involve aircraft and other sophisticated equipment, and air force careers are primarily technical in nature. This means that it provides great opportunities to learn mechanical, electrical, electronic, and other advanced technical skills that can later be useful in obtaining employment in civilian life. To make the most of learning opportunities in the air force, you need a good grounding in math and basic science. The more advanced your knowledge is in these areas, the better your chances of obtaining a desirable position.

This book begins with a look at the process of enlistment and basic training. It then describes various careers available in the air force. The last chapter takes a brief look at the services available to those who have served, after they leave the U.S. Air Force.

CHAPTER 1

ENLISTING IN THE AIR FORCE

The air force is the branch of the U.S. armed forces responsible for air and space missions, including protection against enemy aircraft attack, surveillance, and air transport. It is also responsible for monitoring nuclear threats and providing protection against nuclear attack.

The air force is one of the most elite of the armed forces. Because it does not employ large numbers of troops on the ground and many of its activities require the use of aircraft and complex equipment, it primarily needs recruits with technical skills. Therefore, it is very selective in whom it accepts. In addition, it processes recruits into active service as the need for individuals with particular skills arises. Being a member of the air force gives a person the opportunity to learn valuable technical skills while serving one's country.

BASIC REQUIREMENTS FOR ENLISTING

To enlist in the air force, you must be at least eighteen years old, or seventeen with parental consent, and not more than twenty-seven years old. Individuals up to age thirty-four can enlist in the Air Force Reserve. Exceptions to the upper age limit are sometimes made for those with previous military experience.

Enlistment in the air force requires a high school diploma. Very few recruits are accepted without one. You must be a U.S. citizen or a permanent legal resident of the United States. Further, the air force requires recruits to be in good physical condition and to be of good character.

To enter the air force, you must achieve a qualifying score on the Armed Services Vocational Aptitude Battery (ASVAB). Each branch of the service has its own acceptable score to qualify a recruit for enlistment, and the air force's score is one of the highest. The ASVAB is structured similarly to the SAT. It has a number of sections covering different aptitudes. The sections are:

- Arithmetic Reasoning (AR)
- Mathematics Knowledge (MK)
- Word Knowledge (WK)

- Paragraph Comprehension (PC)
- Assembling Objects (AO)
- Auto and Shop (AS)
- Electronics Information (EI)
- General Science (GS)
- Mechanical Comprehension (MC)

As you can see, achieving a good score on the test requires solid knowledge of math and science. Many of the careers in the air force are highly technical, requiring airmen to perform electrical, electronic, and mechanical tasks. Your ASVAB score determines which categories and levels of careers are open to you. Thus, the more you know in these subjects, the greater your career options will be.

Indeed, knowledge and education, especially in science and math, are of paramount importance in the air force. For this reason, you may be able to enter active duty with a higher rank if you have completed at least twenty semester hours of college credit. Completing a three-year high school Junior ROTC program or earning specific awards in organizations such as the Civil Air Patrol, Boy Scouts, or Girl Scouts may also entitle you to enter service at a higher rank.

The air force offers two enlistment programs: the Guaranteed Training Enlistment Program, which guarantees a particular job, and the Aptitude Area Enlistment Program, which guarantees a general skill

Recruiters from the 477th Fighter Group answer questions and provide information. Recruiters provide information to those interested in joining the air force and keep reservists' information up-to-date.

area. More information on the specific achievements required for these programs can be obtained from an air force recruiter.

If you think you would be interested in learning more about a career in the air force, you should talk to a recruiter at your local military recruitment center or contact an air force recruiter through the Web site (http://www.airforce.com). If you are interested in entering the U.S. Air Force Academy as a cadet, you can contact admissions through the Web site (http://

www.usafa.af.mil). Ask all the questions you can think of, and then think about the commitment you will need to make. Are you cut out for military life and the possibility of combat? If you feel that a career in the air force is right for you, and the air force recruiter has prequalified you, you will make a date to report to a Military Entrance Processing Station (MEPS).

STRUCTURE OF THE AIR FORCE

The U.S. Air Force is divided into functional groups called commands. These commands are similar to divisions in a large corporation. Each is responsible for overseeing and managing a major area of air force activity. The different commands are:

- Air Combat Command: The largest command, responsible for fighting operations.
- Air Education and Training Command: Responsible for the recruitment, training, and educational activities of the air force.
- Air Force Matériel Command: Responsible for research, development, and evaluation of equipment and weapons systems.
- Air Force Space Command: Responsible for missile systems.
- Air Force Special Operations Command: Controls special operations, such as pararescue and Battlefield Airmen.

- Air Force Mobility Command: Responsible for transporting forces, airlift operations, and in-air refueling of aircraft.
- Pacific Air Forces: Responsible for air and space operations in the Pacific region.
- United States Air Forces in Europe: Based in Europe, this command is responsible for combat, humanitarian, and peacekeeping operations abroad.
- Air Force Reserve Command: A corps of part-time airmen.
- Air National Guard: Primarily concerned with maintaining security and assisting with disasters in the United States.

ENLISTED

E-1	E-2	E-3	E-4	E-5	E-6	E-7	E-8	E-9	E-9
no insignia							Senior Master Sergeant (SMSgt)	Chief Master Sergeant (CMSgt)	Command Chief Master Sergeant (CCM Sgt)
Airman Basic (AB)	Airman (Amn)	Airman First Class (A1C)	Senior Airman (SrA)	Staff Sergeant (SSgt)	Technical Sergeant (TSgt)	Master Sergeant (MSgt)	First Sergeant (E-8)	First Sergeant (E-9)	Chief Master Sergeant of the Air Force (CMSAF)

First Sergeant (E-7)

OFFICER

O-1	O-2	O-3	O-4	O-5	O-6	O-7	O-8	O-9	O-10	
2nd Lieutenant (2nd Lt.)	1st Lieutenant (1st Lt.)	Captain (Capt.)	Major (Maj.)	Lieutenant Colonel (Lt. Col.)	Colonel (Col.)	Brigadier General (Brig. Gen.)	Major General (Maj. Gen.)	Lieutenant General (Lt. Gen.)	General (Gen.)	General of the Air Force General of the Army (reserved for wartime only)

The air force is further divided into units called wings. Each wing contains four squadrons. A squadron consists of ten to twenty of a particular type of plane, such as bombers, fighters, or transport planes.

Enlisted ranks are airman basic, airman, airman first class, senior airman, staff sergeant, technical sergeant, first sergeant, chief master sergeant, and chief master sergeant of the air force. Officer ranks are second lieutenant, first lieutenant, captain, major, lieutenant colonel, colonel, brigadier general, major general, lieutenant general, general, and general of the air force.

THE ENLISTMENT PROCESS

When you go to the MEPS, you need to bring your Social Security card, driver's license, and birth certificate. If you have earned any college credits, bring the transcripts with you. If you have any certificates for special skills such as flight training, bring those as well. You should remove any piercings and wear appropriate and comfortable clothing. Do not wear sandals or open-toed shoes, tank tops or sleeveless shirts, or shirts with offensive sayings. Bring your eyeglasses or contact lenses. Do not bring expensive jewelry or other valuables. Electronic devices such as CD players, iPods, smartphones, and tablet and laptop computers will be secured during processing.

This example of the ASVAB test (http://www .asvabprogram.com/index.cfm?fuseaction=overview. testsample) illustrates the types of questions that appear on the actual test.

You should get a good night's sleep, have a good breakfast, and arrive early. Processing is often an all-day process. If there is no MEPS near you and you have to travel a significant distance, you may be authorized to stay in a hotel the night before processing, at the government's expense. Lunch is provided at the MEPS free of charge, and dinner will be provided if you require overnight lodging.

THE OATH OF ENLISTMENT

All members of the armed forces are required by federal law to take an oath of enlistment, which commits them to joining the military. The first oath of enlistment dates back to the Revolutionary War. Today, the oath is typically administered at an enlistment ceremony, which family and friends are invited to attend. The following is the oath sworn by enlistees in the air force:

I, _____, do solemnly swear (or affirm) that I will support and defend the Constitution of the United States against all enemies, foreign and domestic; that I will bear true faith and allegiance to the same; and that I will obey the orders of the President of the United States and the orders of the officers appointed over me, according to regulations and the Uniform Code of Military Justice. So help me God."

(Title 10, U.S. Code; Act of May 5, 1960, replacing the wording first adopted in 1789, with amendment effective October 5, 1962)

If you have already taken the ASVAB in high school or at an air force recruitment center and achieved qualifying scores, you do not have to retake the test. Otherwise, the first step is to take the ASVAB.

Next, you must pass the physical exam. During the exam, the following tests and measurements will

Air force recruits recite the oath of enlistment at a ceremony at the Indianapolis Motor Speedway. Recruits are sometimes ceremonially sworn in at major sporting and other public events.

be performed: height and weight, hearing and vision, urine and blood tests to screen for medical disorders, drug and alcohol tests, and muscle group and joint maneuver testing. Additional testing or medical consultation may be required if there are any questions about your fitness for service.

After passing the physical, you will meet with an air force liaison, who will explain the enlistment job selection process. The jobs for which you are eligible are based on your ASVAB score, job preferences, physical abilities, and the date that you are available to enter the air force. You will be asked to pick one area for which you are qualified, which will be guaranteed. In that area, you will be asked to pick up to five jobs. However, you will not be assigned a particular job during processing. The job you are ultimately assigned will depend on what is needed and available at the time you are ready for assignment. Next, you will be fingerprinted and given a background check. During this process, you will be asked some personal questions about your marital status and any children you may have, drug or alcohol abuse, legal violations, and concealment of any physical problems.

You will then enter the Delayed Entry Program (DEP) as a member of the Air Force Inactive Reserve. The DEP commits you to report to basic training at a point in the future. The purpose of the program is to provide you with time to prepare for basic training. The time before you enter active duty can range from two weeks to one year. While you are in the DEP, you take part in regular meetings with your recruiters and other recruits. During these meetings, you'll receive information that will help you succeed in basic training and technical school. You will also participate in team-building recreational activities.

10 QUESTIONS TO ASK AN

AIR FORCE RECRUITER

1. What is involved in joining Junior ROTC or regular ROTC in college?

2. Given the academic courses I've taken and my previous experience, what types of jobs would I be likely to qualify for?

3. If I want to qualify for a higher-level or more advanced job in the air force, what additional courses should I take before enlisting?

4. What careers are available in my area of interest?

5. Are there military programs that will help me pay for college prior to enlisting?

6. What are the physical fitness requirements I must meet?

7. What is it like to work in a combat area?

8. Do I have any say in where I will be stationed?

9. What is basic training like?

10. Given my educational background, skills, and previous experience, am I eligible for any special programs or a signing bonus?

Even though you are not on active duty, you are still a member of the air force while in the DEP. It is very important that you maintain your physical fitness while waiting for assignment to active duty so that you will be able to succeed in basic training. If necessary, your recruiter will give you a fitness improvement plan. When you are matched to a specific job in the air force, the MEPS liaison will contact your recruiter, who will inform you what your job will be and when you must report for basic training.

CHAPTER 2

BASIC TRAINING AND SKILL TRAINING

All new air force trainees are sent to Lackland Air Force Base in San Antonio, Texas, for basic training, which takes place in groups of about fifty. Basic training includes orientation, initial war skills, combat lifesaving, threat awareness, physical fitness, airmanship, and a graduation ceremony.

BASIC MILITARY TRAINING

Basic training takes place over eight and a half weeks. It is designed to instill a "warrior mentality" in trainees to prepare them for the rigors of the Air Expeditionary Force (AEF). It also challenges trainees physically and mentally to build up a sense of strength and self-confidence.

The first week of basic training is referred to as Week 0 and is devoted to orientation, evaluations and inspections, and flight drills. During Week 0, trainees are given haircuts and are issued clothing and

A master sergeant encourages a recruit at the end of the low crawl course during basic training. Master sergeants play a key role in training recruits.

equipment. They also receive initial duty assignments. They learn the basics of drilling and how to maintain one's dorm and possessions. The next week, Week 1, is devoted to learning the basics of air force life. Activities and topics include reporting and saluting, nutrition and fitness, individual drills, the laws of armed conflict, and the warrior role. Trainees are issued an identity card and an M-16 rifle. They also receive a briefing on educational benefits and are given appointments for any medical or dental care they require.

Week 2 emphasizes combat skills and personal fitness. Trainees learn basic security and defensive fighting techniques. They undergo dorm inspection and flight drills. They also receive career guidance from human relations. Week 3 covers lifesaving skills for use in combat, including self-aid and buddy care under fire. Skills include applying bandages, dressings, and tourniquets; splinting fractures; and dealing with head wounds, chest wounds, and internal bleeding. Physical fitness training continues, and trainees engage in job interviews.

Week 4 focuses on threat awareness. Topics covered include chemical, biological, radiological, nuclear, and enhanced conventional weapons (CBRNE) training; antiterrorism training; and security programs. Trainees go through more physical fitness training and do the obstacle course, which tests their endurance and fear of heights, confined spaces, and water. They also receive a weapons evaluation, which tests their skills in the breakdown and assembly of weapons.

The work of Week 5 is known as Ready Warrior Training. Trainees undergo Combat Arms Training and Maintenance (CATM), including exposure to M-16 live fire. They learn about mental preparation for combat, basic leadership, and basic situational awareness. They practice self-defense techniques using pugil sticks—heavily padded, polelike weapons. Additional topics include predeployment preparation, military citizenship, and joint warfare (operations involving forces from multiple services). They also explore issues related to the media and public relations.

Week 6 is considered the most demanding week of basic training. During this week, trainees experience the BEAST, or Basic Expeditionary Airman Skills Training. Trainees are put to the test in realistic combat scenarios and training exercises that use all the skills and tactics they have learned. They also undergo Survival, Evasion, Resistance, and Escape (SERE) training, in which they learn what to do if they are captured by enemy forces. Finally, they receive a post-operation critique and a deployment briefing.

During Week 7, evaluations are performed, and trainees receive information on air force history, combat stress recovery, sexual assault prevention and reporting, suicide awareness and prevention, and financial management. As in the other weeks, they continue physical fitness training. Finally, trainees reach Week 8—graduation. They receive a technical school briefing to prepare them for the academic courses related to their assigned careers. They also participate in the graduation ceremony and receive their orders.

EDUCATION IN THE AIR FORCE

Training is not over when one completes basic training. The next step is to participate in technical training, which takes place at specific air force bases. Technical

This staff sergeant is an aerospace propulsion systems craftsman. He is inspecting the exhaust nozzle of an F-16 Fighting Falcon at Spangdahlem Air Base, Germany.

training takes a few weeks to a year or more, depending on the career. It takes place at an appropriate air force base in three phases. Upon the completion of each phase, an individual receives more privileges.

Today's air force is high-tech and requires personnel who understand mechanical, electronic, and physics principles and techniques. Therefore, education is of primary importance in the air force. Every enlisted person attends the Community College of the Air

Force (CCAF), which provides college-level courses. All enlisted airmen take required courses that can lead to an associate's degree in a technical field, such as aircraft maintenance, electronics and telecommunications, logistics, allied health, metals technology, and information technology. In addition to required courses, airmen can voluntarily take additional courses in their off-duty time. Having an associate's degree in a technical area is of great help in getting a job in technical, scientific, or health fields once one reenters civilian life. It can also shorten the time it takes to get a bachelor's degree, if one attends a four-year college after serving. The following sections describe some of the other educational opportunities provided by the air force.

U.S. AIR FORCE ROTC

The air force offers an ROTC (Reserve Officers' Training Corps) program at nearly one thousand colleges and universities across the United States. The program offers a path to earn a commission as an officer in the air force. The U.S. Air Force ROTC (AFROTC) provides one- to four-year scholarships to both high school and college students who demonstrate outstanding academic and leadership qualities. The scholarships provide partial or full tuition and a nontaxable monthly stipend. In addition, some colleges provide ROTC cadets with an additional subsidy for tuition, fees, and books.

Students in the ROTC make a commitment to
a certain number of years of military service after
graduation. The length of the commitment differs
according to one's career field. Most cadets must
make a four-year commitment to active duty, but
pilots must fulfill a ten-year commitment following pilot training. The air force maintains a Web site
(http://www.afrotc.com) devoted to information about
AFROTC opportunities.

EDUCATIONAL OPPORTUNITIES FOR AIRMEN

The U.S. Air Force provides an excellent opportunity
to get a free college education. The Air Force Tuition
Assistance program, available to all active-duty personnel, pays for academic or technical college courses
taken by airmen and officers in their off-duty time.
If you plan to attend college using student loans and
then decide to enter the air force, be aware that the
air force has a college loan repayment program. The
program will repay up to $10,000 of student loans
accumulated prior to entering the service. However,
you must sign up for this program when you sign
your enlistment contract.

The air force also provides a variety of higher-
education programs for enlisted airmen that can
lead to becoming a commissioned officer. One such

LIFE IN THE AIR FORCE

Air force bases are small, self-contained towns with their own stores and recreational facilities, as well as housing. Enlisted airmen live in dormlike accommodations. Each person has his or her own room and bathroom. There are common recreation rooms and kitchens, where airmen can cook meals. Single officers and families live in houses on base. Those who live off base are provided with a set housing allowance. Members who are stationed internationally receive assistance in relocating their families.

Base facilities rent equipment for camping, boating, and other outdoor activities; these items can be used for off-duty recreation. There are also gyms and facilities for other sports, often including golf, football, basketball, volleyball, swimming, squash, and bowling. Military bases have their own safety, fire, and security (police) personnel.

Air force bases have a staff that works with the families of active-duty personnel. When airmen are stationed away from their families or in combat zones, various resources are available to help their families. Services range from childcare facilities to assistance from human resources personnel in acquiring all the benefits to which the family is entitled. Mental health counselors help in dealing with stress and emotional issues. The Airman and Family Readiness Center on base provides practical assistance to the airmen's spouses and families. Several military Web sites and online support groups assist families as well.

program is the Airman Education and Commissioning Program (AECP). Those who qualify for the AECP remain on active duty but are assigned to an AFROTC detachment. Their job is to go to school as full-time college students. The airmen selected for this program receive a scholarship for tuition and fees and a textbook allowance. They participate for up to three years, depending on their degree programs and previous academic history. The AECP is available only for specific majors, including nursing, meteorology, physics, math, most engineering majors, and certain foreign language and foreign-area studies specialties. All AECP students entering the program, except nurses, will go on to complete commissioning training through the Basic Officer Training (BOT) course at Officer Training School (OTS) after earning their bachelor's degrees. Nurses attend the Commissioned Officer Training (COT) course.

The Airman Scholarship and Commissioning Program (ASCP) is available to selected airmen, who are given the opportunity to earn a commission as an officer while they complete their bachelor's degree as ROTC cadets. They are released from active duty and enlisted in the Air Force Reserve. They receive the same tuition-and-fees scholarship and textbook allowance as in the AECP. ASCP scholarships are available for two to four years in a variety of fields, including technical, nontechnical, nursing, prehealth, and foreign language areas. They are also available for graduate studies. Graduates receive a commission as a second lieutenant and are returned to active duty for at least four years.

In the Professional Officer Course: Early Release Program, active-duty airmen who can complete all bachelor's degree and commissioning requirements within two years can receive an early release from active duty to enter the AFROTC. The program is open to students in all majors. Selected airmen separate from the active duty force, join an AFROTC detachment, and become full-time college students. After achieving a bachelor's degree, they are commissioned as second lieutenants. They return to active duty for at least four years. Students do not collect military pay and benefits while in the program.

Officers also have an opportunity to enhance their education by earning graduate degrees. The air force has its own graduate school, the Graduate School for Engineering and Management, located at Wright-Patterson Air Force Base in Ohio. This school, which is part of the Air Force Institute of Technology (AFIT), allows officers to advance their careers by obtaining a master's degree or Ph.D. in more than twenty specializations. Arrangements can also be made for officers to obtain advanced degrees in other specializations at civilian colleges and universities.

The AFIT provides advanced educational opportunities through its Center for Cyberspace Research

(CCR), which conducts defense-focused research at the graduate level. In addition, the air force offers the Technical Degree Sponsorship Program (TDSP), which is available to those working on an engineering or meteorological degree. This program allows participants to earn money while completing their college education. It's available to engineering and meteorological students who are within twenty-four months of graduation. Candidates must successfully pass an evaluation by an OTS board. After selection, candidates receive active-duty E-3 (airmen first class) enlisted pay along with housing and food allowances, as well as medical and dental benefits. After graduating, they are commissioned as officers and placed in an air force job that utilizes their technical skills.

THE U.S. AIR FORCE ACADEMY

The U.S. Air Force Academy trains students, called cadets, to become officers in the air force. To enter the academy directly, applicants must be recommended by a congressman, senator, or the vice president of the United States. Information on admissions can be found on the academy's Web site (http://www.academyadmissions.com/#Page/Getting_in_the_Academy). The academy provides instructions to interested students to help with the nomination process.

The first step is to start preparing while still attending junior and senior high school. Prepare by

Cadets in the class of 2014 salute during the playing of the "Star-Spangled Banner." The swearing-in ceremony marks their first full day of basic cadet training at the Air Force Academy.

choosing appropriate academic courses and engaging in physical fitness training. The air force recommends taking the following high school courses (and aiming for above-average grades):

- Four years of English, including a college-prep composition course
- Four years of math, including algebra, geometry, trigonometry, and calculus

- Four years of science, including chemistry, physics, computer science, and other science courses
- Two years of social sciences, including history, economics, and government
- Two years of a foreign language

The air force offers an admissions application package with detailed admissions guidelines and physical fitness requirements, which may be available from your high school guidance counselor or air force recruiting station.

Leadership Encouraging Airman Development (LEAD) is an air force program that encourages commanders to seek out promising airmen for admission to the U.S. Air Force Academy, where they can be trained to become officers.

The Academy Preparatory School is designed to prepare qualified young enlisted men and women to enter the U.S. Air Force Academy. It is located on the academy grounds and is a ten-month school that provides intensive academic, physical, and mental preparation. The school's program covers the four areas of training provided by the academy: academics, military training, athletics, and character development. Students, known as cadet candidates, study math, English, and general sciences.

CHAPTER 3

AVIATION AND TECHNICAL CAREERS

The air force uses a wide variety of aircraft, from those that deliver equipment and supplies to stealth aircraft encompassing the most advanced technology available. It also maintains a variety of specialized aircraft, including helicopters, small planes, and remotely piloted vehicles. Keeping all aircraft in top condition and repairing them when necessary is critical to the success of combat, surveillance, and support missions. Therefore, the air force provides a wide range of apprentice positions for new recruits. In these positions, enlisted airmen learn trades and engineering principles while working with high-tech equipment.

This chapter describes some of the hands-on technical jobs that must be filled to keep aircraft flying and ready for missions. The list of careers provided here and in the next few chapters is not exhaustive. The air force offers more than 140 different career

The Northrop B-2 Spirit stealth bomber is designed to evade enemy radar through the use of flat surfaces, radar absorbent materials, and hidden engines and weapons.

options. It should, however, give you a feel for the types of high-tech jobs available in the modern air force. Additional information on these and other careers can be found at the U.S. Air Force Web site (http://www.airforce.com).

This chapter examines a number of positions in aerospace and flight technology. Positions related to direct combat are described in the next chapter.

KEEPING AIRCRAFT FLYING

Aerospace maintenance apprentices perform scheduled inspections, functional checks, and maintenance on all kinds of aircraft and aircraft-installed equipment. There are a variety of specialized positions in particular technical specialties. For example, aviation propulsion apprentices work on and test engines. Electrical and environmental systems apprentices work on electrical and electronic systems, such as ignition, steering, and pressurization systems. Aerospace fuel systems apprentices work on fuel systems, tanks, and cells. All of these areas provide valuable electrical and/or mechanical skills.

In addition to maintaining the systems in aircraft, maintaining and repairing metal components is necessary. This is the job of those in aircraft metals technology. Apprentices evaluate broken parts, draw working sketches, make templates, consult shop drawings, and select materials. They perform machine

A senior airman performs maintenance on an aircraft. Many careers in the air force allow airmen to develop electrical and electronic skills that can later be applied in civilian jobs.

tool-cutting operations and use engine lathe-cutting gears, slots, keyways, and other work pieces. They weld metal using a variety of methods. Materials include cast iron, carbon steel, copper, copper alloys, ferrous alloys, aluminum, magnesium, titanium alloys, nickel, and cobalt base alloys.

The aircraft maintenance officer plans, manages, and oversees all aircraft maintenance operations, including the loading of ordnance (weaponry). This

AIRMAN'S CREED

This is the Airman's Creed, which represents an individual's commitment to colleagues and country:

> I am an American airman.
> I am a warrior.
> I have answered my nation's call.
>
> I am an American airman.
> My mission is to fly, fight, and win.
> I am faithful to a proud heritage,
> A tradition of honor,
> And a legacy of valor.
>
> I am an American airman,
> Guardian of freedom and justice,
> My nation's sword and shield,
> Its sentry and avenger.
> I defend my country with my life.
>
> I am an American airman:
> Wingman, leader, warrior.
> I will never leave an airman behind,
> I will never falter,
> And I will not fail.

officer also develops flight and aircraft maintenance schedules and procures resources required to keep aircraft operational.

Avionics

The air force offers a career in integrated avionics technology, as well as positions in avionics systems for specific aircraft. In this field, individuals operate and maintain avionics systems, which are the electrical and electronic systems that operate the aircraft. They work on radar, integrated test systems, built-in-test (BIT) equipment, recording systems, and video display systems, among others. Part of the job is to inspect avionics systems and software to make sure they are operational. They also prepare aircraft for low-altitude attack profiles, precision bombing, covert operations, and reconnaissance. Some in this position are given the role of the aircraft's dedicated crew chief.

Air Traffic and Airport Control Careers

Air traffic controllers are critical to the success of air force missions. They perform a variety of complex duties in control towers and radar facilities to keep aircraft taking off, landing, and flying in an orderly and safe manner. This position requires both technical knowledge and the ability to interact well with other professionals who have information necessary for controlling flights. Air traffic controllers use two-way radio communications, radar systems with associated computer equipment, landline communications systems, and visual light-gun signals to control the flight of aircraft.

This is a high-pressure job. Air traffic controllers must not only perform routine control of aircraft, but also provide emergency assistance to aircraft and notify and coordinate with emergency personnel when necessary. Controllers also work with air weather service personnel by making limited weather observations and relaying pilot-reported weather conditions. In addition to guiding military aircraft, air force air traffic controllers provide air traffic control services to commercial and private aircraft. They are certified by the Federal Aviation Administration (FAA) for this purpose. Thus, many of the skills gained in this job are transferable to comparable positions in the civilian sector. Air force controllers work very closely, often in the same facility, with civilian controllers or civil aviation authorities in other nations. Air traffic controllers receive a degree in airway science from the CCAF.

People in airfield management, starting as apprentices, work at U.S. airfields worldwide to ensure pilots' ability to safely land, take off, and taxi. They are trained in how to operate, manage, and inspect

An air force air traffic controller with the 100th Operations Support Squadron adjusts flight progress strips used to track each aircraft's flight data.

airfields and monitor airfield construction projects. They are among the primary responders to in-flight and ground emergencies. Individuals in airfield management also check flight plans, en-route weather, and notices for other locations. They transmit flight plans and flight movement messages to air route traffic control centers, flight service stations, and control towers. This job often requires apprentices to work multiple shifts in order to support flying operations and ensure the mission readiness of the air force throughout the free world.

The airfield systems field covers the various systems required to operate an airfield. These include meteorological, navigational, and air traffic control ground-to-air radio systems. Those in this field deploy, maintain, and modify such systems. They are responsible for flight inspection of navigational aids.

Airfield operations officers are responsible for overall management of the airfield. In addition to running airfield operations, they interface with the FAA.

CHAPTER 4

COMBAT, LAW ENFORCEMENT, AND EMERGENCY CAREERS

This chapter examines the role of air force personnel in combat, in both direct and indirect combat roles. The Air Combat Command (ACC) is central to the air force. Roughly two-thirds of personnel are in the ACC. The air force offers a wide range of combat positions, many of which provide training in electrical, mechanical, and other technical skills, in addition to combat skills. Airmen who specialize in combat positions go on to receive advanced tactical and combat training after completing basic training.

DEFENSE, COMMAND, AND CONTROL CAREERS

Surveillance is an important part of defense. Aerospace control and warning systems personnel, starting as apprentices, operate ground-based radar and command and control systems. There are two primary radar systems: the Joint Surveillance System (JSS) and the Ground Theater Air Control System (GTACS). The JSS consists of permanent installations; its primary goal is the defense of the continental United States and Canada. The GTACS consists of mobile facilities that can be moved anywhere in the world. It is used for defense and in support of military operations wherever necessary.

Managing global military missions is an enormous task. Command post positions are located in air force operations centers around the world. At command posts, personnel use telephone networks, radio communications, computers, and alerting systems to control operations and maintain communication with other centers. They direct the takeoff of aircraft and monitor their locations, keeping commanders throughout the air force advised of the status of the aircraft.

People stationed at a command post could be working at a base with only a few aircraft, at one with missiles as well as aircraft, at the headquarters of a major command, or at air force headquarters. Some command post apprentices even operate aboard aircraft as aircrew members. Other command post personnel operate equipment that controls the launching of missiles. When there are emergencies involving aircraft, civil disasters (such as an explosion that affects a city's infrastructure), or other events that affect national security, command post personnel execute action plans and follow orders to deal with them. Because these positions are so critical, the standards for selecting command post apprentices are very high.

When engaging in a mission, armament is often of key importance. Aircraft armament systems apprentices are responsible for inspecting, preparing, and repairing weapons systems in all sorts of aircraft. They work with bombs, ammunition, and missiles. Apprentices may be stationed in an operations or maintenance crew. Or, they may be assigned to the Air Force Matériel Command at Elgin Air Force Base, where they test and evaluate new and prototype weapons and weapons systems. Others are stationed at the Air Force Special Operations Command, where they work with specialized aircraft, such as AC-130 gunships and small aircraft.

AIRBORNE CAREERS

Let's face it: one of the major reasons that people join the air force is that they want to fly. While the first career that typically comes to mind is piloting, this is an officer position, which requires a college degree. There are several different types of pilots, including fighter pilots, bomber pilots, test pilots, tanker pilots, helicopter pilots, trainer pilots, reconnaissance/surveillance/electronic warfare pilots, special operations pilots, and remotely operated vehicle pilots.

Maj Jason Forest

The pilot of an F-15C Eagle prepares for takeoff at Nellis Air Force Base in Nevada. He is participating in the Joint Expeditionary Force Experiment, a biannual test of new military technologies.

Being a pilot involves a lot more than just flying a plane. In addition to flying aircraft, the pilot commands the aircrew. Also, pilots must learn a wide range of mathematical and scientific information and technical procedures in order to perform their role.

Piloting is not the only flying career. There are a variety of other positions in the aircrew, and these are open to qualified enlisted personnel. One such area is airborne battle management systems. Not all radar and sensing equipment is land-bound. Airborne battle management systems apprentices are part of the aircrews that operate airborne warning command and control systems. These include computerized airborne radar sensors and electronic countermeasure equipment.

After academic training, personnel in this area receive flight training, after which they are assigned to an operational squadron. Then they receive additional training in procedures necessary to operate in various theaters. They may be assigned to overseas units and fly on E-3 or EC-130 aircraft, or they may be assigned to bases within the continental United States.

Beginning as apprentices, aerial gunners operate weapons systems and related equipment on board aircraft employed around the world. They also perform scanning duties, using night-vision goggles. Aerial gunners are trained in electrical, mechanical, and hydraulic technology.

Airborne cryptology is another flying specialty. In addition to performing regular aircrew responsibilities, airborne cryptology apprentices use equipment such as radio receivers and recording equipment to perform airborne signals intelligence functions. Airborne cryptologists send and receive coded messages and capture, translate, evaluate, and report on communications for intelligence purposes. They also keep track of information related to mission aircraft, targets, and orders.

CAPTAIN EDWARD RICKENBACKER

The U.S. Air Force boasts one of the most well-known Congressional Medal of Honor winners of all time, World War I flying ace Captain Edward "Eddie" Rickenbacker. Before joining the air force, Rickenbacker was a racecar driver. He participated in the Indianapolis 500 several times before World War I.

In 1917, Rickenbacker joined the aviation section of the Signal Enlisted Reserve Corps as a sergeant first class. He was sent to the aviation headquarters of the American Expeditionary Force in France. His mechanical skills made him valuable, and he was assigned to a flight school as an engineer. However, he was not allowed to train as a pilot because his education was considered inadequate. He practiced flying on his own at the flight school where he was stationed. Eventually, he was allowed to join a fighter aircraft unit and train. He was commissioned as a first lieutenant.

In 1918, Rickenbacker was assigned to the renowned 94th "Hat-in-the-Ring" Squadron.

The following month, he shot down his first German plane. Barely four months after joining the squadron, Rickenbacker had shot down five planes, making him an ace. In September 1918, he was pro-moted to captain and took command of the 94th Squadron. He continued to command the squadron until January 1919.

Rickenbacker returned to the United States as the leading U.S. ace, with twenty-six confirmed victories over the enemy. He was awarded numerous French and U.S. decorations, including the French Legion of Honor (chevalier) and two Croix de Guerre medals, with Palm. He was awarded the Congressional Medal of Honor "for conspicuous gallantry and intrepidity above and beyond the call of duty in action against the enemy near Billy, France, Sept. 25, 1918." While on patrol over the lines, Lieutenant Rickenbacker attacked seven enemy planes (five German Fokkers, protecting two Halberstadts). Despite the odds against him, he dived on them and succeeded in shooting down one of the Fokkers and one of the Halberstadts.

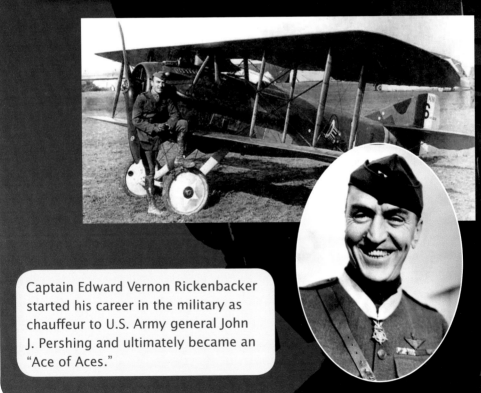

Captain Edward Vernon Rickenbacker started his career in the military as chauffeur to U.S. Army general John J. Pershing and ultimately became an "Ace of Aces."

Airborne intelligence, surveillance, and reconnaissance (ISR) operators capture, evaluate, and manage a wide range of information from aboard aircraft. They manage both airborne and ground-based ISR processing systems. Their job is to warn of potential threats and assist with mission planning. They are often stationed in combat theaters and work with tactical-level operations to provide information to those involved in military operations.

AIR BATTLE MANAGERS AND COMBAT SYSTEMS OFFICERS

There are a variety of combat officers in addition to those who are pilots; they provide the planning, supervision, and management of particular areas. Air battle managers plan and oversee aviation operations on board aircraft, including managing air defense, combat, and tactical missions. They fly on aircraft including E-3 AWACs, E-8 Joint-STARs, and the Airborne Laser. They also analyze national defense objectives, create operational policies, and conduct flying and simulated exercises to maintain operational readiness.

Combat systems officers (CSOs) manage combat operations. They are employed in a range of specialties. Bomb and fighter CSOs manage electronic warfare and weapons functions during combat missions. Test CSOs plan and direct programs that test new and

A gunner in the 82nd Airborne Division patrols in a Black Hawk helicopter in Iraq, searching for guerrilla strongholds.

modified aircraft, aerospace vehicles, and flight simulators. Trainer CSOs oversee all levels of CSO training. Reconnaissance/surveillance/electronic warfare CSOs plan and manage missions to accomplish search and rescue, electronic combat, reconnaissance, and surveillance missions. Mobility CSOs plan and manage operations to move resources where necessary for military operations. Tanker CSOs perform duties related to air refueling. Remotely operated aircraft (ROA) CSOs operate unmanned vehicles for reconnaissance and combat purposes. Special operations CSOs manage special ops training and missions.

The air liaison officer (ALO) commands Tactical Air Control Party (TACP) and Air Support Operations Center (ASOC) operations. The ALO coordinates air, space, and cyber capabilities with ground force army commanders for use with U.S. and coalition forces. The ALO works in battlefield areas and is trained for all forms of combat, including the use of advanced technology and weapons systems.

Combat rescue officers lead teams for search-and-rescue missions in combat areas. They also organize and train search-and-recovery personnel and help plan special reconnaissance missions.

DEMOLITION AND SPECIAL FORCES CAREERS

The Air Force Special Operations Command (AFSOC) has four main responsibilities:

- Forward presence and engagement. (This involves moving into an area in advance of military action, often with the goal of having personnel in place in case military action later becomes necessary.)

- Information operations (intelligence).
- Precision employment and strike.
- Special operations forces mobility.

In addition to carrying out combat and special missions, the AFSOC is also involved in search-and-rescue operations, as well as humanitarian operations when necessary.

A job in special operations is often the first career that young people think of when they consider joining the military. These are some of the most exciting positions in the air force. They can also be fulfilling because the missions are usually of critical importance. However, the reality is that they are also the most dangerous and carry the highest risk of death or injury.

In addition, the physical demands of qualifying for such a position are so great that a large number of people who try out fail to complete training. If you apply and are accepted for such training and wash out, this may adversely affect your career. So you need to be very certain you are up to the demands of training before you apply. These positions are for people with enormous physical prowess as well as high intelligence and technical aptitude. The following sections describe some of the special operations positions in the air force.

An air force videographer films an explosive ordnance disposal team using radio detonation to explode unspent munitions seized from insurgents in Iraq.

Explosive Ordnance Disposal

Explosives are a fact of life in combat, and the air force requires experts who are capable of dealing with them. Explosive ordnance disposal (EOD) apprentices train to become EOD technicians. EOD technicians know how to safely handle live explosives. They use classified techniques and special procedures to detect, identify, render safe, recover, and dispose of explosives and unsafe ordnance (ammunition and

NUCLEAR WEAPONS

Nuclear weapons are part of the U.S. military arsenal and require experts to deal with them. Nuclear weapons apprentices are trained in all aspects of this weaponry. They learn how to inspect, assemble, and disassemble nuclear weapons. They maintain, repair, and modify them. They test a variety of ordnance, including missiles, bombs, and reentry vehicles and systems. Those in this position are trained in a number of systems, including the air-launched cruise missile and the short-range attack missile. They may also be given introductory training on the Minuteman and Peacekeeper intercontinental ballistic missile reentry systems.

other supplies). This profession is demanding and dangerous, but it can be very satisfying because EOD technicians are involved in saving lives.

Explosives that EOD technicians are trained to work with include conventional military ordnance; homemade devices created by criminals and terrorists; and chemical, biological, and nuclear weapons. EOD technicians also analyze unknown munitions and explosives for the intelligence agencies. They support the U.S. Secret Service in the protection of the president, vice president, and other dignitaries. Candidates must complete rigorous training that requires determination and motivation.

Tactical Air Control Party (TACP)

There are fewer frontline combat positions in the air force than other services. However, the Tactical Air Control Party (TACP) is one unit that is involved in frontline combat. For this reason, at the time of this writing, the TACP apprentice position is available only to males, as are other special forces positions described in this section. This is an elite group, and members wear a black beret bearing the TACP flash and crest.

Every TACP mission has strategic implications, so this is a position with demanding technical and intellectual, as well as physical, requirements. Members of the TACP are trained to read maps and use a compass; target enemy locations; use survival, escape, and evasion techniques; engage in small unit tactics; employ camouflage techniques; and carry out operations in hostile environments. They are also trained to master a variety of weapons. They learn to operate and maintain cutting-edge technology, including communications and computer systems, digital networks, and targeting and surveillance equipment. Among the special-purpose tactical vehicles they operate in the field are Stryker combat vehicles, High-Mobility Multipurpose Wheeled Vehicles (HMMWV), and Mine-Resistant, Ambush Protected (MRAP) vehicles.

Individuals in this position work with the U.S. Army as well as the U.S. Air Force. They are responsible for

Tactical Air Control Party (TACP) members train with the army to ensure wartime readiness. In this training exercise, one airman provides small arms cover for another, who drags a "casualty" to safety.

providing the army and allied forces with tactical air support. Support is provided from both the ground and aircraft, such as the A-10 Thunderbolt II, B-1B Lancer, and Unmanned Aircraft Systems. TACPs are responsible for managing close-air support missions in the battle area to support ground operations.

TACPs are usually assigned to air force units stationed with conventional ground combat units, including armored and infantry units, as well as airborne and air assault units. Those with sufficient experience and special skills may work with army special operations forces. Typical TACP missions require observing the battle area, identifying hostile targets, pinpointing their locations using high-tech equipment, and attacking targets.

TACPs also perform command and control functions for Air, Space, and Cyber (ASC) missions, working at Army Tactical Operations Centers. After completing technical school, members attend the U.S. Air Force Combat Survival School. They may go on to attend airborne, air assault, Pathfinder, Ranger, HALO (free-fall parachuting), or sniper schools, depending on mission needs. TACP officers' functions are similar to those of air liaison officers, which were described earlier in this chapter.

It is possible to enter the air force with a guarantee to become a TACP. Or, you can apply for TACP while in basic training. However, it is very difficult to meet the academic and physical demands of training to qualify. Before applying, be sure to have the mental as well as physical preparation needed to succeed. In order to be accepted, you must successfully complete the TACP Physical Ability Stamina Test. Candidates must meet the following requirements, obtained from the U.S. Air Force Web site:

- Running: 1.5 miles (2.4 kilometers), or six laps around a 440-yard track, in less than eleven minutes and forty-one seconds
- Push-ups: At least thirty-nine repetitions within a one-minute time limit
- Crunches: At least forty-five repetitions within a one-minute time limit
- Pull-ups: At least two repetitions while striving for six

Other Special Forces Careers

Another elite position is combat controller (CCT). This position is a part of the Battlefield Airmen Air Force special forces. CCTs are combat-ready, FAA-certified air traffic controllers who operate in remote and hostile areas. They are trained as precision parachutists who can penetrate hostile areas. CCTs are also trained in scuba diving and amphibious techniques; driving motorcycles and snowmobiles; and using skis, rappelling, and fast-rope procedures. They receive survival training and can travel overland in any environment. In their role as air traffic controllers, they establish assault zones and direct aircraft.

This is one of the most elite jobs in the air force, but also one of the most dangerous and mentally and physically demanding. As with TACP positions, in order to be accepted, applicants must successfully complete the Physical Ability Stamina Test, which includes the following, obtained from the U.S. Air Force Web site:

- Swimming: Two 20-meter (21 yard) underwater swims and one 500-meter (546 yard) surface swim in fourteen minutes
- Running: One 1.5-mile (2.4 km) run in ten minutes, forty-five seconds
- Pull-ups: Six pull-ups in one minute
- Sit-ups: Forty-five sit-ups/crunches (with hands behind head) in two minutes
- Push-ups: Forty-five push-ups in two minutes

CCT officers plan, organize, and direct the operations of CCTs.

Another special forces position is pararescue. A pararescueman (also called a PJ, for "parachute jumper") is an enlisted combat-ready specialist who performs air force and special operations search-and-rescue functions. These specialists are trained

Airmen perform a high-altitude, low-opening (HALO) parachute jump from a height of 9,500 feet (2,896 meters) to a precise target in a training exercise for combat controllers and pararescuemen.

to parachute into hostile areas and provide aid to survivors as certified emergency medical technicians (EMTs). They also provide aerospace rescue and recovery support for space flights for the National Aeronautics and Space Administration (NASA).

PJs are certified as scuba divers and trained in amphibious procedures, as well as survival skills in a wide range of hostile climates. They learn rappelling, skiing, snowmobiling, and motorcycling. Before being accepted, candidates must pass the Physical Ability Stamina Test and meet the same requirements as those for combat controller positions. The PJ officer's functions are similar to those of the combat rescue officer (CRO), described earlier in this chapter.

Special operations weather personnel support special operations teams. They operate atmospheric measurement instruments and computer workstations, and they retrieve data from radar and weather satellites. They collect information and analyze this data to predict oceanographic, meteorological, and space atmosphere conditions. They also prepare reports on weather advisories, warnings, and inclement environmental conditions. They may be stationed anywhere in the world in all types of climates.

Special ops personnel require special skills to survive in the most dangerous conditions. Survival, evasion, resistance and escape (SERE) specialists teach these skills to special operations personnel. SERE specialists experience the most demanding training in all types of weather conditions and terrain—arctic, desert, ocean, and jungle, among others. They become expert in how to survive in the wilderness, finding their own water, food, and shelter; navigating by map and compass; and providing their own first aid. In addition, they develop special skills in signaling and rescue techniques and in how to evade enemies and escape if they are captured. They also learn how to teach others these skills. SERE specialists train and operate in all major climatic conditions.

FIRE, SECURITY, AND EMERGENCY SERVICES CAREERS

Keeping those living on bases safe requires the same types of emergency services that exist in civilian life. These include firefighters and police, as well as emergency management teams equipped to deal with military emergencies, such as attacks.

Emergency management apprentices keep bases prepared for military attacks and natural disasters and are responsible for responding to such emergencies if they occur. They must be prepared to respond not only to direct or terrorist attacks but also to natural threats, such as hurricanes, tornadoes, floods, and earthquakes. They participate in training exercises and disaster simulations designed to hone their ability to respond effectively. If an attack or natural disaster occurs, emergency management personnel man and operate a mobile command post to relay information to keep the base running and coordinate the emergency response.

Bases have their own fire departments. The job of fire protection apprentices is to save lives and property. Apprentices attend technical school, where they are trained to fight all types of fires, including

U.S. Air Force firefighters train with live fire and simulated aircraft to stay up-to-date in fire and rescue techniques.

those that affect buildings, hazardous materials, and aircraft, as well as miscellaneous fires. They are also trained to fight wild land fires, such as grass and forest fires. They learn to operate fire vehicles and equipment, and they receive Red Cross certification in standard first aid and cardiopulmonary resuscitation (CPR). They also learn principles and procedures for rescue, including the use of special tools to free trapped people.

The security forces carry out all police activities on an air force base. As in the civilian police force, there are many different areas of work. Apprentices in this field learn how to direct vehicles; operate speed-, alcohol-, and drug-testing equipment; and conduct investigations. They are trained in lifesaving procedures as well as armed response because, like their civilian counterparts, they are called upon to help people in trouble and respond to security problems.

Security forces are responsible for catching and holding suspects and securing crime scenes. They are sometimes called upon to testify in judicial proceedings. Security forces personnel also use military working dogs. However, apprentices must complete their initial security training before they are eligible to be selected to work with dog teams.

The skills learned in this area are directly transferable to civilian jobs in law enforcement and security. In fact, the college credits gained from the CCAF can be applied toward a degree in law enforcement. Security forces officers manage the security forces and plan and control security operations. Special investigation officers conduct criminal, fraud, counterintelligence, and internal security investigations. When necessary, they work jointly with other federal agencies, such as the U.S. State Department, Secret Service, and federal counterintelligence and law enforcement agencies.

CHAPTER 5

HEALTH CARE CAREERS

G iven the rigors of military life, as well as the dangers of combat, injuries are common in the military. Medical personnel help heal those injured in the line of duty and treat diseases and disorders experienced by members of the air force and their families. This chapter covers both patient care positions and those that involve technical and laboratory skills.

PATIENT CARE CAREERS

Patient care careers can provide a great deal of satisfaction because you are part of a team that helps heal people. These careers also provide skills that are directly transferable to the private sector.

Aerospace medical services apprentices learn to perform basic medical support duties. They work in inpatient facilities such as hospitals and outpatient facilities such as clinics. They also assist in delivering and caring for newborns. In outpatient settings, they assist physicians by preparing patients for examination and helping with treatments and procedures. Some medical service apprentices work in emergency medicine. They drive ambulances and carry out procedures designed to save lives. In this role, they receive training that allows them to take the National Registry of Emergency Medical Technicians (NREMT) examination.

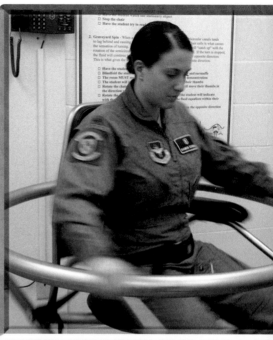

A physiologist with the 359th Aerospace Medical Squadron spins slowly in a Bárány chair, which is used to help prevent airsickness.

Surgical service apprentices learn to assist with patients undergoing surgery, much like civilian surgical nurses. They transport patients to and from the operating room, arrange and count sterile instruments and sponges prior to surgery, and pass them to the surgeon during surgery. They also assist anesthesia personnel when necessary.

Aerospace physiology personnel work to ensure that crewmembers have the skills and preparation to perform at high altitudes in advanced aircraft and spacecraft. At times, rapid changes in air pressure in an aircraft require crewmembers to be treated in a hyperbaric chamber (a chamber in which the air pressure can be raised and lowered). Aerospace physiology personnel provide this treatment and observe crewmembers on board aircraft. In addition, they fit crewmembers with flight suits, maintain the suits, and provide support for high-altitude reconnaissance and air delivery missions. They may also work on research and development activities.

The military employs dental, ophthalmic, and medical assistants to work with air force dentists, optometrists, and physicians. In this role, they maintain records, prepare instruments and materials, and assist dentists and physicians in performing procedures. The skills they learn in these areas are transferable to the same jobs in civilian life.

Physical medicine assistants work with physical therapists in the evaluation and treatment of patients with muscle and bone problems. They administer physical therapy treatments designed to relieve pain and improve muscle and joint functions. They apply electrical devices, ultrasound treatment, heat, cold, water, light, exercise, massage, and traction.

Mental health service apprentices provide mental health services, including inpatient and outpatient treatment and alcohol rehabilitation. They assist

NURSE ENLISTED COMMISSIONING PROGRAM

Nurses are in great demand in the air force. Therefore, the service has a special program called the Nurse Enlisted Commissioning Program (NECP). This program provides active-duty airmen, both female and male, with the opportunity to earn a bachelor's degree in nursing. Students complete the degree at a college or university with an AFROTC detachment or at a college or university with an agreement with the air force. Tuition and fees are paid by the AFROTC detachment. Applicants must have fifty-nine hours of previous college coursework, including general psychology, anatomy and physiology I and II, microbiology, chemistry I and II, nutrition, and statistics.

This program allows airmen to remain on active duty and continue to receive an income while going to school full time. Those selected for the NECP receive scholarships and a textbook allowance. After receiving their nursing license, they are commissioned as officers and attend Commissioned Officer Training and the Nurse Transition Program. The air force also offers advanced training to enlisted nurses through the Physician Assistant Training Program.

psychiatrists, psychologists, social workers, and mental health nurses in planning, evaluating, and providing patient care. They obtain clinical information from patients and counsel patients with professional supervision. Individuals in this position must be

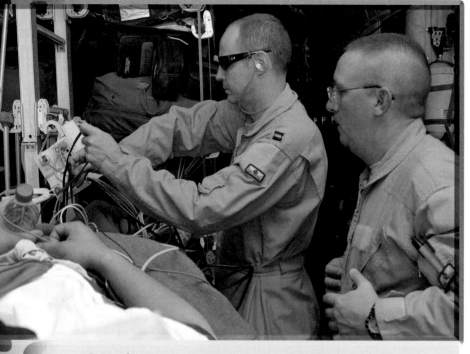

Critical care air transport team (CCATT) members set up medical equipment for a patient inside an aircraft. The team provides intensive care during aeromedical evacuations.

willing to develop a therapeutic relationship with patients. They must learn about the medications used in treating mental illness, including their potential negative effects. Mental health service apprentices may also give and score psychological tests.

Pharmacy apprentices learn to dispense prescriptions in inpatient and outpatient settings. They prepare medications in response to drug orders for hospitalized patients. For medications not available in prepared form from manufacturers, they compound drugs from ingredients. They also prepare medications for injection into patients. In addition, they must safeguard drugs and chemicals in the pharmacy. This career requires a solid background in math because many calculations are required in performing this work.

LABORATORY AND DIAGNOSTIC CAREERS

Laboratory analysis is important in identifying and successfully treating many diseases. The air force employs laboratory technicians trained in:

- Hematology: The medical science that deals with blood
- Immunohematology: The medical science that deals with immune system elements in the blood
- Coagulation: Blood clotting
- Microbiology: The branch of biology that deals with bacteria and viruses
- Parasitology: The branch of biology that deals with parasites
- Serology: The medical science that deals with blood serum
- Chemistry
- Laboratory management

Responsibilities of laboratory technicians include collecting and preparing samples for analysis and then using scientific equipment to test specimens. Clinical laboratory technicians process blood for transfusion and evaluate the blood cells and blood components. Individuals in this position are eligible to become credentialed clinical laboratory technicians by passing the exam from the National Certification Agency for Medical Laboratory Personnel. They can become registered medical laboratory technicians by passing an examination from the American Society of Clinical Pathology.

Histopathology apprentices prepare tissue specimens for microscopic analysis to diagnose disease. They work with both surgical and autopsy specimens. After graduating and meeting the work experience requirements, histopathology apprentices are eligible to take an examination from the American Society of Clinical Pathology to become a nationally credentialed histopathology technician.

Cardiopulmonary laboratory apprentices are trained to assist doctors and other health professionals in diagnosing and treating diseases that affect the heart and lungs. Those in this career are involved in four areas: (1) respiratory therapy, which deals with breathing problems; (2) pulmonary diagnostics, which identify lung problems; (3) invasive cardiology, in which medical devices inside the body, such

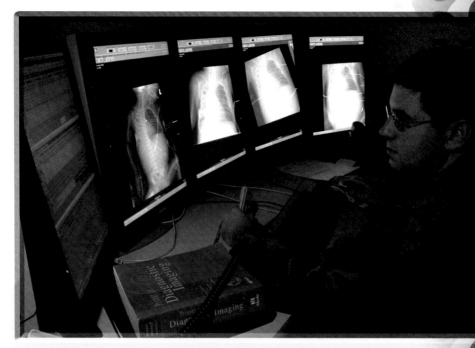

A radiology resident with the 759th Medical Operations Squadron reviews X-rays and dictates findings for a final report to the requesting physician.

as cardiac catheters, are used to treat heart problems; and (4) noninvasive cardiology, in which devices outside the body, such as ultrasound machines and electrocardiograph (EKG) machines, are used to identify heart problems. The training course is accredited. This means that those who graduate can obtain national credentials, which can later be used to qualify for similar positions in the civilian community.

Diagnostic imaging apprentices are trained to work in the radiology department in air force medical facilities. The radiology department helps diagnose diseases by using machines that take pictures of the inside of the body using X-rays or magnetic technology. Apprentices are assigned to a particular subspecialty involving X-ray technology, including radiography (X-ray pictures), computerized axial tomography (CAT) scans, or mammography. Alternately, they can receive special training in imaging with ultrasound, which uses sound waves; magnetic resonance imaging (MRI), which uses electromagnets; or nuclear medicine, which uses radioactive material.

The Diagnostic Imaging Apprentice course is accredited by the Joint Review Committee on Education in Radiologic Technology. Therefore, those who take it are eligible for national certification as a radiologic technologist. Individuals can also obtain an associate's degree through the CCAF by taking several college classes in addition to completing their training.

Dental laboratory technicians are assigned to dental laboratories. They make and repair dentures, metal or porcelain crowns (caps that go over teeth), bridgework, orthodontic devices, mouth guards, and other dental appliances.

Physicians, dentists, psychiatrists, and psychologists become medical, dental, and mental health officers in the air force. They may work in outpatient clinics or hospital settings. They may also be involved in humanitarian missions. Because of the need for physicians, the air force offers three- and four-year scholarships for medical school, which require a three- or four-year commitment to military service, respectively.

PUBLIC AND OCCUPATIONAL HEALTH CAREERS

Health services management personnel perform the administrative functions necessary to run a health care facility. They can work in a variety of areas, including human resources, patient care, admissions, and medical records.

The bioenvironmental engineering career field in the air force combines the responsibilities of the Occupational Safety and Health Administration (OSHA), the Environmental Protection Agency (EPA), and the Nuclear Regulatory Commission (NRC). Those in the field inspect conditions in community and workplace environments and review procedures to keep workers and the community safe. They are also part of the aerospace medicine team.

Using specialized survey instruments and equipment, personnel collect and evaluate samples to identify any hazards that exist in the workplace. Environmental samples are collected to evaluate drinking water, wastewater, air, soil, and other materials. The samples are tested for physical, chemical, radiological, and bacteriological contamination. Personnel also use

During a training exercise, a bioenvironmental engineering technician and an emergency management technician take air and ground radiation readings to determine if people in the area need to be evacuated.

radiation-measuring instruments and review facilities, equipment, and operations to ensure that radioactive material is used and disposed of in compliance with environmental safety and health standards. In addition, they conduct medical readiness surveys in order to identify chemical, biological, and radiological agents and provide advice on their use and safety.

Public health apprentices perform tasks similar to those performed in federal, state, or local public health departments. There are four major areas in this field. The first is communicable disease control, which requires interviewing and educating people about infectious diseases, such as sexually transmitted diseases (STDs), tuberculosis, and hepatitis. Individuals in this area may need to collect, identify, and recommend control of insects, animals, plants, and other elements that might spread disease. The second area is facility sanitation, which involves inspecting food-service and other public facilities to make sure the physical setup and procedures meet sanitary standards. The third area is occupational health. Workers in this area assist in the development of physical exam requirements and educate workers about proper procedures relating to physical, biological, and chemical hazards. It also involves investigating occupational incidents, such as exposure to toxic chemicals. The fourth area is food inspection, which involves the inspection of food to ensure its quality and safety.

CHAPTER 6

SCIENCE AND ENGINEERING CAREERS

The air force's emphasis on technology and infrastructure means that it requires engineers and engineering support personnel. Also, because the air force is involved in a number of scientific areas, from optics to space technology, this branch of the military provides excellent opportunities for those interested in a career in science.

ENGINEERING CAREERS

Engineering positions are held by officers and require a college degree. The air force has programs that assist applicants in attaining a college degree. If you are interested in a career as an engineer, this is one way to defray the costs of obtaining the necessary education.

Civil engineers design, build, and modify the buildings and utilities that form the infrastructure for the air force. They specialize in a particular area, such as architectural, electrical, mechanical, or environmental engineering. Like civilian engineers, their activities involve project management, including planning, budgeting, and supervision; drafting; surveying; performing feasibility studies; and managing construction and utility operations. In the air force, the job may also include disposing of conventional, nuclear, or chemical-biological ordnance (weapons and ammunition). Engineers may also be involved in emergency response in the event of a terrorist attack or natural disaster.

Developmental engineers develop and modify air force systems. They can specialize in any number of engineering disciplines, including aeronautics (aircraft systems), astronautical systems (systems used in spaceflight), computer systems engineering, or electrical and mechanical engineering.

Engineering technicians, who start as apprentices, are enlisted airmen who work in the engineering field. People in this position use conventional construction surveying devices, global positioning systems (GPS), and automated surveying instruments. They work on military construction, including project-mapping operations, construction support surveys, road construction and building, and utility layout surveys. They perform drafting functions manually and with computer-aided drafting (CAD) systems, creating engineering graphics; architectural, structural, and roadway drawings; and map overlays. They also work with geographic data

METEOROLOGY

Weather has a serious effect on the success of military operations and is critical in the case of air missions. Therefore, the U.S. Air Force stations weather personnel throughout the world. They support both air force and army missions. Weather apprentices learn to perform functions similar to those of civilian meteorologists: analyzing weather conditions, forecasting the weather, and issuing weather warnings. In addition, they provide weather information to pilots.

Those who are selected to become air force weather apprentices receive college-level instruction in the basic principles of meteorology. Most weather apprentices work in one of eight operational weather squadrons, which are located around the world. After completing this initial assignment, they are eligible for assignment to a combat weather team that supports an air force flying wing, an army aviation unit, or an army ground combat unit. Alternately, they may be eligible to volunteer for a special ops team or an army unit assignment as a weather parachutist.

Weather officers manage and direct weather operations. They provide information for operations and operational planning. They may also be asked to perform and supervise significant meteorological weather studies and research.

and develop, operate, and maintain modules for the geographic information system (GIS). This system combines data mapping, statistical analysis processes, and database capabilities to provide detailed geographical information.

Other infrastructure-related careers for enlisted airmen include electrical systems and electric power production. Electrical systems personnel start as apprentices and perform tasks similar to those performed by civilian electricians. They install, service, modify, and repair electrical equipment and systems. Electrical power production apprentices learn to install, operate, maintain, repair, and inspect the power plants that provide the energy to keep operations running.

MISSILE AND SPACE TECHNOLOGY

Missile and space systems maintenance personnel maintain the intercontinental ballistic missile (ICBM) systems used to defend the United States. The ICBMs are located in underground, unmanned launch facilities, which are in secret locations across the United States. Enlisted airmen maintain the mechanical systems of the ICBMs and install missile components in them. Those who perform this work have a

A missile maintenance airman works on a Minuteman III intercontinental ballistic missile (ICBM) at F. E. Warren Air Force Base in Wyoming.

top-secret security clearance. Because they can work only at a limited number of facilities, and only in the United States, they are stationed at one place longer than most people in the military. This provides more time for activities such as obtaining a college degree. Another advantage of this career is that once a person reaches skill level 5, he or she has the opportunity to apply for the following positions:

- Space lift maintenance technician at Cape Canaveral in Florida or Vandenberg Air Force Base in California
- Defense threat-reduction agency inspector, who performs inspections to monitor treaty compliance
- Research and development technician
- ICBM test-launch maintenance instructor

The skills learned in these positions can prepare you for logistics manager and defense contractor logistics positions in civilian life.

Spectrum operations technicians are enlisted airmen who analyze and manage broadcast frequencies for terrestrial (land-based) systems, aircraft-based systems, and space systems. They also coordinate radio, radar, and other frequencies. They gain an understanding of wireless communications systems technologies and work with program officers, developers, and potential users of equipment.

Space systems operations personnel, starting as apprentices, assist with spacecraft mission requirements and electronically transmit spacecraft commands. They assist in the design of space mission objectives, working with orbital printouts. They transmit and verify commands and operate data-handling terminals to keep track of spacecraft.

Two officers from the 740th Missile Squadron simulate launching a Minuteman III ICBM in the missile procedure trainer.

Space and missile operations officers manage space and missile operations, working with national and international space agencies on the launching, control, and tracking of ICBMs, spacecraft, and satellites. They manage space and missile combat crew operations and work in command posts for space and missile operations, including those related to positioning satellites and other space-based objects.

SCIENCE

Developing new materials, processes, and devices is the key to a successful modern military. Scientists are officers who work in a variety of exciting areas. They conduct or manage research programs and projects aimed at solving scientific problems and developing new materials and processes. They also serve as technical advisers on scientific and technical boards and committees. Areas for chemists in the air force include fuels, propulsion, and materials; hyperspectral research (an area that studies the use of light waves beyond what can be seen by the human eye); biotechnology testing and evaluation; chemical and biological agent sensors; management of bio-optical detectors; and chemical engineering. For physicists, areas include lasers, nuclear engineering, and optics (the study of light).

The Air Force Institute of Technology (AFIT) offers a variety of advanced degrees for scientists, including imaging science and engineering physics degrees. Scientists tend to either stay in their positions, conducting research, or move on to program management later in their careers.

CHAPTER 7

INFORMATION TECHNOLOGY CAREERS

Latitude > 44° 49'
Longitude > 20° 28

Almost every current movie or television show about the military includes a computer expert, who saves the day by locating critical information or a vital target. In the real world, information technology (IT) is truly critical to the success of missions in the air force. Some of the career training available involves directly working with computer hardware, software, and technology. Other training involves the use of technology in monitoring for intelligence or security purposes. These careers provide a chance to work with the latest technology and learn transferable skills in an area that is critical throughout society.

COMPUTER SCIENCE CAREERS

A variety of computer-related positions at various skill levels exist in the air force. Computer systems operations apprentices learn how to operate and

An air force sergeant in charge of software engineering develops a software program for a precision air strike from an undisclosed location in southwest Asia.

repair computers, receiving hands-on training on PCs, communications equipment, and computer networks. They also learn how to safeguard classified information that is sent and received through the Department of Defense's secure processing network.

Knowledge information management apprentices learn how to manage data, information, and knowledge-sharing services. They perform these functions in both permanent and field positions.

They use technology to collect, organize, and store information.

Computer systems programming apprentices analyze, code, maintain, develop, test, and document computer software for user, network, and database systems. They harness the power of computer systems to collect, process, store, retrieve, analyze, and display data, providing information that is critical to military operations.

Individuals in the cyber transport systems field install, maintain, and troubleshoot networked data, video systems, and cryptographic equipment. They design, configure, operate, modify, and secure networks.

In the cyber systems operations field, systems operators keep the computer networks and systems operational. They install, support, and maintain servers and distributed systems, as well as network storage, messaging, and other computer systems. They must develop plans to deal with service outages and interruptions that might affect the network. They work with networked systems and applications both at bases and at deployed locations. Individuals in this area may also use their expertise to assist in identifying, monitoring, and exploiting computer-based vulnerabilities in systems belonging to those who are hostile toward or a threat to the United States.

Cyber surety is the policing function of IT. Workers in cyber surety monitor users' computers, computer networks, data/voice systems, and databases and protect them from unauthorized activity. They work on systems at bases and are deployed to mission locations. They must detect and resolve security problems and violations. They enforce national, Department of Defense, and air force security policies and directives.

Communications and information officers manage information technology for both fixed and deployed units. They analyze hardware and software needs for networks and systems, and they develop policies, procedures, and standards. In addition, they are responsible for running communications and IT operations.

INTELLIGENCE CAREERS

Knowledge is power, and no mission can succeed without reliable and thorough intelligence. These intelligence-related positions require the use of computer and telecommunications equipment and systems to collect and analyze data.

Network intelligence analysis is part of the signal intelligence career field. Enlisted airmen in this position analyze radio communications, identify communications networks, and interpret radio messages. Another signals intelligence position is communications signals intelligence. Enlisted airmen in this position learn international Morse code and operate receiving and recording equipment. They use classified

An Air Forces Central software engineer discusses how to combine intelligence, surveillance, and reconnaissance information in a combined air operations center.

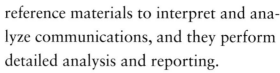

reference materials to interpret and analyze communications, and they perform detailed analysis and reporting.

Cryptologic linguists operate voice communications equipment and electronic equipment to perform frequency searches, and they use direction-finding equipment to identify where signals are coming from. They transcribe recorded voice communications signals and analyze the transcripts. Individuals in this position are generally deployed overseas. They receive training in a particular foreign language and do not necessarily have to know one in advance.

People in the electronic signals intelligence exploitation field operate advanced electronic equipment that monitors, measures, and analyzes special signal transmissions, such as pulsed radar and AM and FM radio transmissions. They operate electronic signal searching, signal collection, and signal-monitoring equipment. They use signal analysis equipment such as oscilloscopes, spectrum analyzers, and analog recorders. Their goal is to identify where radar and other electronic transmissions are coming from

TRACKING WEAPONS OF MASS DESTRUCTION

Technical applications specialists collect and analyze data related to weapons of mass destruction—including nuclear, chemical, and biological weapons—and use data systems to monitor compliance with nuclear treaties. They collect information on research, development, and testing. This information is provided to national agencies, policymakers, and those in combat command.

Technical applications specialists are assigned worldwide and may be deployed in situations ranging from single-person operations to large air force bases. Only a small number of applicants are accepted for this position. Training is intensive, covering a wide range of subjects, including physics, computer technology, math, statistics, and chemistry. Individuals start in entry-level data collection or maintenance jobs, but they can work their way up to management or development jobs using cutting-edge technology. They can ultimately reach the level of detachment superintendent or even attain a policy-level position.

and why they are being sent. This helps them establish whether the transmissions are related to early warning systems or weapons systems. The first would indicate a defensive system, whereas the second would indicate possible offensive weapons. Data collected in this way is used to develop strategies in war and monitor hostile forces throughout the world. This position requires a solid background in basic algebra and math. Although not required, an academic background in areas of science such as physics and some experience with scientific equipment is beneficial.

Sensor operators employ electro-optical (using electricity and light) sensor systems and electronic protection (EP) equipment to collect, record, display, and distribute information related to military missions. They provide support for missions in close-air support, interdiction (continuous bombing for purposes of disruption), armed reconnaissance, and combat search-and-rescue, among others. Their job is to maintain communications with ground, air, and maritime units. They may also perform airborne operations. Among the functions they perform are intelligence, surveillance, and reconnaissance (ISR); basic surface attack (BSA), using precision guided munitions; close-air support (CAS); and real-time battle damage assessment.

The operations intelligence specialty involves collecting, analyzing, and reporting intelligence

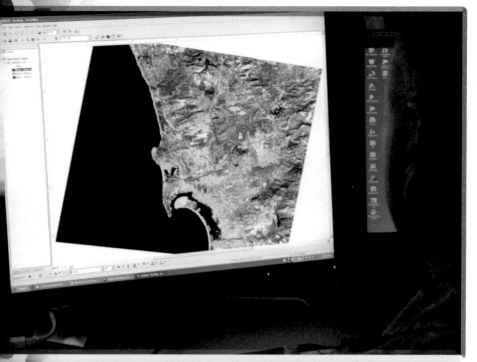

FalconView, Windows-based mapping software, displays a variety of maps and geographical overlays to assist in analyzing terrain. The software displays data obtained from Earth-orbiting satellites.

information to support combat mission planning and execution. Personnel must analyze intelligence information collected from a variety of sources to establish if it is accurate. If it is, it must be distributed to the appropriate areas of command.

Among the systems used to collect intelligence information are automated combat intelligence and message-handling systems, as well as personal computers. Operations intelligence specialists create and maintain databases of information on enemy forces, including their location, equipment, and capabilities. This information aids all levels of command in carrying out missions, including selecting targets and planning attacks. The specialists must brief aircrews and commanders on threats, general intelligence information, and mission-specific intelligence information. They are involved in detailed mission planning and are deployed at both air force and joint service locations throughout the world. When deployed at headquarters level, they provide high-level commanders with the intelligence necessary for decision making. At the operational unit level, they provide intelligence to commanders and mission planners so that they can successfully plan and execute missions.

The intelligence officer is responsible for coordinating the activities of those involved in collecting and analyzing intelligence information. Intelligence officers must provide integrated intelligence information from all sources. They often work jointly with other government agencies, and even with other governments.

Geospatial intelligence functions as the eyes of the intelligence community. They identify, analyze, and report targets captured on film. Aside from analyzing standard optical imagery, they interpret radar, infrared (light waves too short to see with the human eye), and multispectral imagery. They also assist aircrew members engaged in reconnaissance in planning, recovering, and interpreting imagery from tactical aircraft, such as C-130s, U-2s, SR-71s, F-14s, and remotely piloted aircraft (RPA). Imagery information is stored in intelligence databases and used to establish order of battle (OOB), or the arrangement of troops in battle; survey lines of communication (LOCs); establish helicopter landing zones (HLZs); analyze coastal areas for beach landings; identify targets; and assess battle damage. They also prepare imagery interpretation reports.

CHAPTER 8

COMMUNICATIONS, LOGISTICS, AND ADMINISTRATIVE CAREERS

Like any other large organization, the air force requires a large number of administrative personnel to keep things running. This chapter discusses three major organizational areas: communications, logistics, and administration. All of these areas are critical to keeping the air force operating effectively and efficiently.

COMMUNICATIONS CAREERS

Getting the right information to the right people at the right time is critical in operating effectively and efficiently. Information is one of the most valuable resources an organization has. Information management (IM) consists of several divisions: publications, records, and administrative communications. Publications creates and distributes official publications, including regulations, manuals, and forms. The records division manages official records.

An air force photographer with the 4th Combat Camera Squadron takes a picture of children interacting with military personnel in the village of Shabila Kalan in Afghanistan.

Administrative communications is responsible for distributing all mail and electronic communications, including orders, and ensuring document security. Enlisted IM workers may work in any of these areas. They often use electronic information management systems or desktop PCs. They may work with computer graphics as well as text communications.

Getting the right information to the public—the responsibility of the public affairs division—is also an important task. This area is similar to public relations in the civilian arena. Enlisted airmen enter this area as public affairs apprentices. Those in public affairs write and edit news for both internal and civilian newspapers. They develop relationships with local and regional civic leaders to improve military-civilian relations. They put together newspapers, prepare layouts, read and correct proofs, and coordinate the distribution of newspapers.

Radio and television are other important means of disseminating information. Another entry-level communications job in the air force is radio and television broadcasting apprentice. Apprentices in this area work behind the scenes on broadcasts. In addition, the responsibilities of this position include maintaining film and tape libraries. Specific jobs include cameraman, announcer, scriptwriter, narrator, and equipment operator. It is very likely that if you apprentice in this area, you will be stationed overseas.

Despite the prevalence of electronic media, still photography remains an important way to record events. Therefore, the air force offers apprenticeships in still photography. Apprentices study photographic techniques, camera operation, and photo processing. They are taught to use cameras with film sizes of 4 x 5 inches, 120 mm, and 35 mm. They are also taught to do portrait photography using studio lighting techniques and equipment. They may be sent on investigative photographic assignments, in addition to photographing sports, ceremonies, and other activities, where they take action or documentary photos.

The public affairs officer plans and manages public affairs activities. He or she coordinates efforts with government agencies and maintains relationships with civilian and government contacts. Public affairs officers also organize and manage the release of information to the public.

LOGISTICS

Logistics is getting the right resources to the right place at the right time. Air force resources include people, equipment, and supplies. There are two aspects to logistics: planning and distribution. In an entry-level logistics planning position, enlisted personnel support planning processes. They prepare support plans, identify where and when resources are needed, and monitor the deployment of personnel and products.

Contracting personnel are enlisted airmen who buy equipment, supplies, and services to support base activities. They review purchase request descriptions for completeness and determine the best method of contracting for goods or services. They prepare documents requesting quotes or proposals. They then review prices and quotes and prepare orders or contracts.

Materials management personnel start as apprentices and work to get material and equipment to

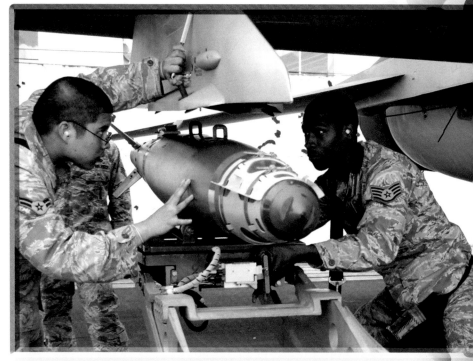

An airman and a sergeant with the 46th Test Wing load a bomb onto an aircraft. Proper handling and distribution of munitions are important for the success of air force missions.

those who need it for air force operations. Materials management apprentices keep track of inventory and perform accounting and financial planning functions related to logistics. They also research and identify supplies and equipment.

Munitions (weapons and ammunition) are the life-blood of any military endeavor. Munitions personnel start as apprentices and are responsible for receiving, storing, maintaining, distributing, and disposing of non-nuclear munitions. They transport munitions in a variety of vehicles. This career field provides wide-ranging experience: it involves computer operation, operations and inventory management, heavy equipment maintenance, electronics, managing personnel, and other skills. Munitions personnel have the opportunity to work with the latest air force jet fighters and bombers and can be stationed anywhere in the world.

Logistics officers are responsible for logistics and policy planning; aircraft, missile, and space airlift maintenance; inspection; and command and supervision of logistics operations. Logistics readiness officers are responsible for materials management and the distribution of materials and equipment, including planning to get supplies to combat troops. Contracting officers manage the acquisition of supplies and services. They organize and oversee the contracting process.

ADMINISTRATIVE CAREERS

Administrative positions in the air force are similar in concept to their civilian counterparts. However, the specific details relate to supporting military operations, as opposed to civilian activities.

As in any organization, human resources (HR) is a major function. Enlisted personnel in this field maintain personnel records through both manual and computerized systems. They advise personnel on career development. They discuss career-related matters, including job specialties, special assignments, promotions, training and retraining programs, and duty selection. They process personnel for separation from the air force, as well as for reenlistment, changes of routine, and special duty assignments.

One aspect that differs from civilian human resources activities is assisting, advising, and counseling military personnel and their dependents on military matters that affect them. Because they or their family members may be deployed overseas, with some airmen working in dangerous environments, HR personnel help them deal with the practical aspects of a difficult and stressful situation. They also advise them about the military-specific programs available to them.

Personnel and manpower officers manage the human resources area. They develop policies, implement programs, and ensure that needs for personnel are met.

No organization runs effectively without control of its finances. The area that controls finances in the air force is the financial management comptroller field. Enlisted personnel in this position maintain records relating to accounting control, commercial services, material costs, and real estate. To do this, they use both manual and automated systems. They monitor the funds available for purchasing and verify the accuracy of amounts billed and paid. They prepare budgets and monitor operating costs, payments to

SPECIAL CAREERS

One specialty career field in the air force is legal affairs. The air force employs lawyers at the officer level called judge advocates. They work in the full range of legal areas, including criminal, contract, international, environmental, medical, space, labor, and property law. The legal branch of the air force is involved in issues across the globe.

To support the legal function, the air force requires paralegals, who are enlisted airmen. Paralegals help the advocates who provide legal services to clients. They also counsel commanders and other leaders on a variety of legal issues. Their duties are similar to those of civilian paralegals. Their work involves administratively processing cases, conducting legal research, interviewing witnesses and victims, and drafting opinions and documents. Most paralegals are members of the active-duty force who have entered the field through retraining. However, a limited number of paralegals are interviewed and selected during basic military training. Once a person is selected for paralegal training, he or she attends the para- legal apprentice course at the Air Force Judge Advocate General's School at Maxwell Air Force Base in Alabama.

Another specialty career is chaplain. Chaplains are officers who perform religious services and provide religious support to members of the air force and their families. They may be stationed anywhere from a stateside air force base to a combat zone.

The air force maintains both the Premier Band, which is a large marching band, and small regional bands, which play all types of music, including jazz, rock, country, and classical. Members of the air force band perform at ceremonies, parades, and concerts. Members of the band are enlisted personnel. Band officers choose music, manage band operations, and direct the band.

Although not strictly a career, the World Class Athlete Program (WCAP) is a two-year program that allows high-level athletes to devote themselves to training and participating in major national and international events, such as the Olympics.

The United States Air Force Band, formed in 1941, has various units, including the Concert Band, Ceremonial Brass, Chamber Players, Air Force Strings, and the Airmen of Note jazz ensemble.

vendors, and other transactions. They prepare reports and presentations related to finances. Work in this area requires accuracy and attention to detail.

The financial management officer leads the financial management area and is responsible for budgeting, planning, policies, and supervision. Another office related to financial management is that of cost analysis officer. Cost analysis officers perform studies of air force structures, systems, and programs to evaluate their cost-effectiveness.

The services career field is similar to the hotel and restaurant management field in civilian life. Personnel in the services field work in a range of areas. They operate fixed and portable food facilities and equipment, and they plan and prepare meals. They oversee housing for base visitors and operate income-producing ventures. Some are involved in fitness activities, providing fitness training and demonstrating techniques. They may also be assigned to mortuary affairs, which involves helping the families of the deceased with the transportation and disposition of remains, including arranging military honors, escorts, and gravestones and plaques. The services officer is responsible for planning, organizing, and directing the operations of the services area.

CHAPTER 9

LIFE AFTER MILITARY SERVICE

There comes a time when every member of the air force must return to civilian life, whether after a single tour of enlistment or at retirement after a long career. The Department of Defense has established the Transition Assistance Program (TAP) to help members of the armed forces return to civilian life. The Active Duty Preseparation Guide can be accessed on the program's Web site (http://www.turbotap.org) or obtained in print from the Airman and Family Readiness Center on base.

IMPORTANT STEPS

When separating from the military, be sure to get a copy of your records, including medical records. Always retain your discharge papers. Decades after separation from the service, you will still be eligible for certain benefits, such as services at Veterans Administration health care facilities and burial benefits.

Many air force veterans are eligible for treatment for medical disorders at Veterans Administration hospitals located around the United States.

The first issue for most airmen separating from the air force is finding a place to live. There are a number of programs available to help servicemen relocate, including the Relocation Assistance Program and the Spouse Employment Assistance Program. Information is available from the Airman and Family Readiness Center. Veterans' benefits include a home-loan guarantee program that allows veterans to purchase a home without a down payment.

Many veterans are entitled to health care from Veterans Administration facilities. The Airman and Family Readiness Center can assist you with arranging additional health insurance coverage for your family and life insurance, too.

Additional support services are available to veterans who were disabled because of military service, including mobility and assistive equipment and devices, medical care, and vocational training. Veterans with service-related disabilities may also be eligible for disability payments or pensions.

Those who serve in the armed forces for at least twenty years are eligible for retirement pay once they leave the military, as well as continuing medical care.

The second major concern after finding a place to live is finding a job. Many medical, IT, administrative, and technical jobs in the air force are essentially the same as in the civilian community. Other positions do not have direct equivalents, but their basic technical

POST-TRAUMATIC STRESS DISORDER (PTSD)

Post-traumatic stress disorder (PTSD) is an issue of particular importance to military personnel. This combination of psychological and physical symptoms results from exposure to life-threatening and high-stress situations. Symptoms include sleeplessness, flashbacks, nightmares, anxiety, depression, and substance abuse.

The Veterans Administration operates the National Center for PTSD, which provides a wide range of resources for dealing with the disorder. Treatment is available through Veterans Administration facilities.

skills are used in many civilian jobs. The question is how to locate appropriate jobs that use the skills and credentials you have gained in the air force.

TAP provides a variety of information to assist airmen in finding civilian jobs, including programs for locating government jobs; jobs banks, including a special one for defense contractors who wish to hire military personnel; employment counseling; and résumé-writing services. It also provides job training for those who need additional skills. For military personnel who wish to start their own businesses, the Small Business Administration offers the Patriot Express Pilot Loan Initiative.

EDUCATIONAL ASSISTANCE

One of the major reasons people join the military is to pay for college. The Montgomery GI Bill provides veterans with up to thirty-six months of benefits that can be used for degree and certificate programs. The benefits can also be used for flight training, apprenticeship or on-the-job training, or correspondence courses.

A second educational assistance bill was passed after the terrorist attacks of 9/11. The Post-9/11 Bill provides financial assistance for up to thirty-six months for education and training pursued after August 1, 2009. The benefits can be used for undergraduate or graduate degree programs, vocational and technical training, tutorial assistance, books, supplies, and monthly housing. In most cases, benefits can be used for fifteen years following release from active duty. They may also be transferable to spouses or dependent children. Courses you have taken at the CCAF may be transferable to a college program for academic credit. If you have received an associate's degree from the CCAF, this may shorten the time it takes you to earn a bachelor's degree.

AIR FORCE RESERVE

Many veterans remain members of the Air Force Reserve. The Air Force Reserve has many of the same careers found in the regular air force. Members

Members of the Air Force Reserve can be called to active duty when needed. These Fighter Wing reservists are returning from serving in Iraq.

generally train one weekend each month, and once a year they engage in two weeks of continuous training. Members of the active reserve may be called upon to serve whenever and wherever additional forces are needed. They can be deployed to areas ranging from combat zones to the sites of natural disasters.

The air force provides many members with a sense of belonging and of doing something important, which is hard to leave behind. In the words of First Lieutenant Vincent Jardine, a retired air force pilot:

I know what it feels like to be a football player playing in his last game. The game is over, but he does not want to leave the field. If he leaves the field, he has to take off his uniform. If he takes off his uniform, he loses his identity. He's not a linebacker anymore, or a right tackle, or a punt returner. He is just another guy who used to play football. He has lost the only real identity he has ever had. The only identity he ever really wanted.

What does he do now? He has had the "highs." Probably the biggest he will ever have. He is still very young. He tells himself: "It'll be fine." It may be OK, but it probably won't be fine. He has done things he will never be able to do again. He has had emotions he will never have again. He has had feelings he will never have again. He has been part of a group unlike any other group he will ever belong to. He has shared experiences that he can never share with anyone again.

How do I know all these things? One day I had to take off my wings.

GLOSSARY

aeronautics The study of flight.

apprentice An enlisted person receiving specialized training.

astronautical Relating to the study of spaceflight.

cardiac catheter A device inserted into the heart to diagnose and treat disease.

close-air support Military action from aircraft to protect ground forces from attack by enemies nearby.

commission A document conferring the position or rank of an officer in any of the armed forces.

computerized axial tomography (CAT) A method of scanning the inside of the body using X-rays.

cryptographic Having to do with the computerized encoding and decoding of information.

cyber Computer-related.

deploy To move to a strategically useful location.

electrocardiograph A device used to record and analyze heartbeats.

electro-optic Using a combination of electricity and light.

geographic information system (GIS) A computer system that captures, analyzes, and stores geographic information.

global positioning system (GPS) A system of satellites that provide location information to receiving systems on Earth.

hyperbaric chamber A chamber whose air pressure can be adjusted to treat disorders caused by exposure to high pressure.

hyperspectral Dealing with wavelengths of light beyond those visible to the human eye.

infrared A wavelength of light too short to be visible to the human eye.

intelligence In military terms, information about the enemy.

intercontinental ballistic missile (ICBM) A missile that is capable of traveling from one continent to another.

interdiction Continuous bombing designed to sow disorder.

logistics The science of the movement, supplying, and maintenance of military personnel and equipment in the field.

magnetic resonance imaging (MRI) A means of taking pictures of the inside of the body using electromagnets.

multispectral Relating to both visible and invisible wavelengths of light.

munitions Weapons and ammunition.

nuclear medicine The branch of medicine that uses radioactive material to diagnose and treat disease.

ophthalmic Related to the eye.

optics The science of light and lenses.

orbital Relating to the path that objects take around Earth.

order of battle The arrangement of troops in battle.

ordnance Military supplies, including weapons, ammunition, combat vehicles, and equipment.

personnel The people employed in an organization or for a service or undertaking.

radiography Using X-rays to take pictures of the inside of the body.

rappelling The process of climbing down a mountain by means of a rope.

reconnaissance The process of searching for information that is useful for military purposes.

signal intelligence The collection and analysis of signals, such as electronic, radar, or radio transmissions, that indicate that communication is taking place or equipment is operating.

terrestrial Relating to or located on Earth.

ultrasound A method of obtaining images inside the body by means of sound waves.

FOR MORE INFORMATION

Air Combat Command

Public Affairs Office

115 Thompson Street, Suite 211

Langely Air Force Base, VA 23665-1987

(757) 764-5014

Web site: http://www.acc.af.mil

This office provides information on Air Combat Command activities.

Air Force Reserve Command

Public Affairs Office

255 Richard Ray Boulevard

Building 220, Suite 137

Robins Air Force Base, GA 31098

(478) 327-1753

Web site: http://www.afrc.af.mil

This office provides information on Air Force Reserve activities and opportunities. The Web site provides news, history, and information on joining the reserves.

Civil Air Patrol (CAP)

105 South Hansell Street

Building 714

Maxwell Air Force Base, AL

36112-6332

(877) 227-9142

Web site: http://www.capmembers.com

This organization provides information on becoming a CAP cadet and joining as a member, as well as providing services to existing members.

National Museum of the Air Force

1100 Spaatz Street

Wright-Patterson Air Force Base, OH 45431

(937) 255-3286

Web site: http://www.nationalmuseum.af.mil

The museum offers historical exhibits, lectures, and outdoor aviation events. The Web site offers a virtual tour of the museum's exhibits.

U.S. Air Force Academy

2304 Cadet Drive, Suite 2300

USAF Academy, CO 80840

(800) 443-9266

Web site: http://www.usafa.af.mil

The U.S. Air Force Academy provides information on application requirements, academics and training programs, and the Air Force Academy Prep School.

U.S. Department of Defense

1400 Defense Pentagon

Washington, DC 20301

(703) 571-3343

Web site: http://www.defense.gov
This organization provides information on U.S. military activities and specific branches of the military, as well as information for members of the armed forces.

U.S. Department of Veterans Affairs

810 Vermont Avenue NW

Washington, DC 20420

(202) 273-5400

Web site: http://www.va.gov
This organization provides information on benefits for veterans of the military.

WEB SITES

Due to the changing nature of Internet links, Rosen Publishing has developed an online list of Web sites related to the subject of this book. This site is updated regularly. Please use this link to access the list:

http://www.rosenlinks.com/cod/afor

FOR FURTHER READING

Camelo, Wilson. *The U.S. Air Force and Military Careers* (U.S. Armed Forces and Military Careers). Berkeley Heights, NJ: Enslow Publishers, 2006.

David, Jack. *Air Force Air Commandos*. Minneapolis, MN: Bellwether Media, 2009.

Dolan, Edward F. *Careers in the U.S. Air Force* (Military Service). New York, NY: Marshall Cavendish Benchmark, 2010.

Goldish, Meish. *Air Force: Civilian to Airman* (Becoming a Soldier). New York, NY: Bearport Publishing, 2011.

Hearn, Chester G. *Air Force: An Illustrated History: The U.S. Air Force from the 1910s to the 21st Century*. Minneapolis, MN: Zenith Press, 2008.

Holmstedt, Kirsten A. *The Girls Come Marching Home: Stories of Women Warriors Returning from the War in Iraq*. Mechanicsburg, PA: Stackpole Books, 2009.

Huetter, Ted, and Christian Gelzer. *Edwards Air Force Base* (Images of Aviation). Charleston, SC: Arcadia Publishing, 2010.

Lewis, W. David. *Eddie Rickenbacker: An American Hero in the Twentieth Century.* Baltimore, MD: Johns Hopkins University Press, 2005.

Martin, Matt J., and Charles W. Sasser. *Predator: The Remote-Control Air War Over Iraq and Afghanistan: A Pilot's Story.* Minneapolis, MN: Zenith Press, 2010.

Porterfield, Jason. *USAF Special Tactics Teams* (Inside Special Operations). New York, NY: Rosen Publishing, 2008.

Powers, Rod. *ASVAB for Dummies.* 3rd ed. Hoboken, NJ: Wiley, 2010.

Pushies, Fred J. *U.S. Air Force Special Ops* (Military Power). St. Paul, MN: Zenith Press, 2007.

Sandler, Michael, and Fred J. Pushies. *Pararescuemen in Action* (Special Ops). New York, NY: Bearport Publishing, 2008.

Schemo, Diana. *Skies to Conquer: A Year Inside the Air Force Academy.* Hoboken, NJ: Wiley, 2010.

Vanderhoof, Gabrielle. *Air Force* (Special Forces). Broomall, PA: Mason Crest, 2011.

Van Wormer, Nicholas. *The Ultimate Guide to Air Force Basic Training: Tips, Tricks, and Tactics for Surviving Boot Camp.* El Dorado Hills, CA: Savas Beatie, 2010.

Zobel, Derek. *United States Air Force.* Minneapolis, MN: Bellwether Media, 2008.

BIBLIOGRAPHY

Air Force Historical Studies Office. "Captain Edward Vernon Rickenbacker." Retrieved January 28, 2011 (http://www.airforce-history.hq.af.mil/PopTopics/MOH-bios/Rickenbacker.html).

Air Force Reserve. "Air Force Reserve: Who We Are." Retrieved January 15, 2011 (http://afreserve.com/?:Who%20We%20Are).

Air Force Services Agency. "Air Force World Class Athlete Program." USAFSports.com, October 2010. Retrieved January 28, 2011 (http://www.usafsports.com/WCAP.htm).

Benton, Jeffrey C. *Air Force Officer's Guide*. 35th ed. Mechanicsburg, PA: Stackpole Books, 2008.

Nicolls, Boone, and Wayne A. Valey. *Airman's Guide*. 7th ed. Mechanicsburg, PA: Stackpole Books, 2007.

Schading, Barbara, Richard Schading, and Virginia R. Slayton. *A Civilian's Guide to the U.S. Military*. Cincinnati, OH: Writer's Digest Books, 2007.

Tyson, Ann Scott. "Air Force Pararescue Team Plucks Stragglers." *Washington Post*, September 8, 2005. Retrieved January 15, 2011 (http://www.washingtonpost.com/wp-dyn/content/article/2005/09/07/AR2005090702038.html).

U.S. Air Force. "Enlisted Careers." Retrieved January 1, 2011 (http://www.airforce.com/opportunities/enlisted/careers).

U.S. Air Force. "U.S. Air Force Enlisted Opportunities." EA-10-001, recruiting brochure.

U.S. Air Force. "Warrior Fact Sheet." Retrieved January 22, 2011 (http://www.airforce.com/pdf/warrior_fact_sheet.pdf).

U.S. Army Center of Military History. "Oaths of Enlistment and Oaths of Office." Retrieved January 14, 2011 (http://www.history.army.mil/html/faq/oaths.html).

U.S. Department of Defense. "Transition Assistance Program." TurboTAP.org, 2011. Retrieved January 30, 2011 (http://www.turbotap.org).

U.S. Department of Veterans Affairs. "National Center for PTSD." Retrieved January 30, 2011 (http://www.ptsd.va.gov).

INDEX

N

nuclear weapons apprentices, 55
Nurse Enlisted Commissioning Program (NECP), 69

O

oath of enlistment, 16
Officer Training School (OTS), 29, 31

P

pararescuemen/parachute jumpers, 60–62
patient care careers, 66–71
pilots/piloting, 45–46
Post-9/11 Bill, 111
post-traumatic stress disorder, 110
public and occupational health careers, 75–77

R

ranks, enlisted and officer, 14
Rickenbacker, Edward, 48–49

S

scientists, 85
security forces apprentices, 64–65
special operations weather personnel, 62

survival, evasion, resistance and escape (SERE) specialists, 62–63

T

Tactical Air Control Party (TACP) positions, 56–59, 60
technical applications specialists, 92
Technical Degree Sponsorship Program (TDSP), 31
technical training, 24–26
Transition Assistance Program (TAP), 107, 110

U

U.S. Air Force
dangers/drawbacks of joining, 6
reason for joining, 5–6
responsibilities of, 8
structure of, 12–14
U.S. Air Force Academy, 11–12, 31–33
U.S. Air Force Reserve, 9, 13, 29, 111–113
U.S. Air Force ROTC (AFROTC), 26–27, 29, 30, 69

W

weather apprentices/officers, 80
World Class Athlete Program (WCAP), 105

ABOUT THE AUTHOR

Jeri Freedman has a B.A. from Harvard University. She is the author of more than thirty young adult nonfiction books, many published by Rosen Publishing, including *The U.S. Economic Crisis, American Debates: Privacy Versus Security,* and *American Debates: Civil Liberties Versus Terrorism.*

PHOTO CREDITS

Cover (top photo), pp. 1 (top photo), 46 Ethan Miller/Getty Images News/Getty Images; cover (bottom left), pp. 1 (bottom left), 3 (left), 61 U.S. Air Force/Master Sgt. Lance S. Cheung; cover (bottom middle), pp. 1 (bottom middle), 37, 82 Air Force Global Strike Command; cover (bottom right), pp. 1, 25 (bottom right) U.S. Air Force/Airman 1st Class Nick Wilson; back cover U.S. Air Force/Airman 1st Class Jack Sanders; interior graphics (camouflage pattern), chapter openers Shutterstock; p. 5 U.S. Air Force/Staff Sgt. Manuel J. Martinez/ DefenseImagery.mil; p. 11 U.S. Air Force/Staff Sgt. Andrea Knudson; p. 13 Department of Defense; pp. 15, 49, 90–91 U.S. Air Force; interior graphics (silhouette) U.S. Navy/Mass Communication Specialist 2nd Class Mark Logico; p. 17 U.S. Air Force/Daniel Elkins; p.19 © www.istockphoto.com/Russ Lickteig; p. 22 Jerry Lara/San Antonio Express-News/Zuma Press © 2006 San Antonio Express News; p. 32 U.S. Air Force/ Mike Kaplan; p. 35 Ross Harrison Koty/Stone/Getty Images; p. 41 U.S. Air Force/Senior Airman Ethan Morgan; pp. 51, 108, 112–113 © AP Images; p. 54 Petty Officer 2nd Class Brian L. Short/www.dvidshub.net; p. 57 U.S. Air Force/Senior Airman Carolyn Viss; p. 64 U.S. Air Force/Karen Abeyasekere; p. 67 U.S. Air Force/Brian McGloin; p. 70 U.S. Air Force/ Senior Airman Melissa B. White; p. 73 U.S. Air Force/Master Sgt. Kimberly Yearyean-Siers; p. 76 U.S. Air Force/Staff Sgt. Keith Ballard; p. 84 U.S. Air Force/Senior Airman Benjamin Stratton; p. 87 U.S. Air Force/Senior Airman Kasey Zickmund; p. 94 U.S. Air Force/Master Sgt. Kate Rust; p. 98 U.S. Air Force/Staff Sgt. Christine Jones; p. 101 U.S. Air Force/Samuel King Jr.; p. 105 Steve White, CIV/DefenseImagery.mil.

Designer: Les Kanturek; Editor: Andrea Sclarow; Photo Researcher: Marty Levick